What Lies Beneath

poems by

Pamela Hirschler

Finishing Line Press
Georgetown, Kentucky

What Lies Beneath

Copyright © 2019 by Pamela Hirschler
ISBN 978-1-63534-899-6 First Edition
All rights reserved under International and Pan-American Copyright Conventions. No part of this book may be reproduced in any manner whatsoever without written permission from the publisher, except in the case of brief quotations embodied in critical articles and reviews.

ACKNOWLEDGMENTS

Many thanks to the following journals, anthologies, and websites in which versions of these poems first appeared:

The Heartland Review: "After Reading Gary Snyder" and "On the Trail to Rainbow Falls"
Kudzu: "How to Remember" and "The Sum of the Parts."
The Pikeville Review: "The Concert"
Pine Mountain Sand & Gravel: "Transplant"
See How We Are and Lexington Poetry Month Blog: "Scission"
Still: The Journal: "When It's Late"
Talking River: "In defense of Small Towns," "On Learning," and "Appalachia Elegy"
This Wretched Vessel: "What Lies Beneath"

Publisher: Leah Maines
Editor: Christen Kincaid
Cover Art: Sheri L. Wright
Author Photo: Emma Lanter
Cover Design: Leah Huete

Printed in the USA on acid-free paper.
Order online: www.finishinglinepress.com
also available on amazon.com

Author inquiries and mail orders:
Finishing Line Press
P. O. Box 1626
Georgetown, Kentucky 40324
U. S. A.

Table of Contents

And How Does This Remain 1

Remembering 2

Scission 3

When It's Late 4

Remembering 5

After Reading Gary Snyder 6

The Language of Flowers 7

The Sum of the Parts 8

A Poem about You 10

On Learning 11

Appalachia Elegy 12

At the End of Winter 13

To the Man Who Saved the Fledgling This Morning 14

The Concert 15

Orange Beach, Gulf Shores, September 2010 16

Transplant 17

In Defense of Small Towns 18

In the Frame 19

Sky Gazing 20

On the Hiking Trail to Rainbow Falls 21

What Lies Beneath 22

For Christina, Jennifer, Melissa, James, Valerie, your beloveds, and all the grands.

And always, for Bruce.

And How Does This Remain

I can still see the snake—
dead and dry with its head
lifted, mouth open,
tongue waiting
in the roadbed clay.

The house,
a crumbled foundation,
a black and white tiled floor,
and a lilac guarding the old well.

Your grandmother's peonies
bloom over her stillborn child,
and you begin your leaving.

I see the moonbeam through your ribs,
your heart blood drips
on the porch.

Remembering

is what keeps us alive
after we're gone.

We pass down the same path
thousands of times in one lifetime,

the molecules of our breath
mixing with those that came before

the weakness of our silver trapped,
our bags bent by the rain.

Rented rooms stables lockboxes
keep the possessions that chain us

to the life rungs of ladders
hung sideways on walls.

Encounters with bank tellers, priests, babies,
pickpockets, librarians, street performers—

the only evidence we sat on sun-warmed benches,
sang lullabies, drew peacocks with sidewalk chalk.

But the past—and the future—
stands on uneven ground:
polite and misunderstood.

Remembering is what keeps me alive
long after you're gone.

Scission

So much depended on the hand of a girl—
eyes closed, finger on a map,
bus schedule, emptied bank account.

She could not divine
the consequence of choice,
only recognized the intolerable.

Perhaps the mystic knows
whether she chose wrong, or not at all,
stood still, severed from herself.

When It's Late

I turn on the porch light,
tuck regret away where
memory cannot reach,

watch the moon arc
the screened window

as song birds yield to tree frogs.

When it's late,
things undone tug
to the beat of fan blades.

I remember when we slept
under stars, and night creatures crept
beyond the circle of firelight.

Remembering

The sun shines whether I get out of bed or not.
Water drips from the spring when I am not thirsty,

walls keep people out and keep people in
until they don't.

You say dandelions taste good deep-fried
but I've never tried them.

Inertia inhabits me like a corpse
left to decay in a copse of trees

devoured bit by bit by swarms of insects
until the skin itself boils with their teeming

and the eyes, the eyes, the eyes are taken first.

After Reading Gary Snyder

> *Throwing away the things you'll never need*
> *Stripping down*
> *Going home.*
> —Gary Snyder in "Three Worlds, Three Realms, Six Roads"

For hours, I researched every word I did not know,
looked up Eridanus—river of stars
that sprang from a rocky hillside.

I dreamed my brother came to me
in the post office parking lot: a black crow,
big as a chicken or an urn. With his head cocked sideways
he looked at me with our father's accusing eye, said go
find the body and the jar of knurled coins.
He limped on the wire slung low above my car,
spoke to me as only a crow can speak.
I watched a long time with stamps in my hand,
wished I understood—busy, drove away.

Today—another parking lot—
he rips at a paper bag with a thick beak.
He has not driven a car since the seventies,
left it, like most things, behind. I do not know why
he idles in parking lots, idles in parking lots,
when he could fly.

The Language of Flowers

Tulips border the front steps, planted
by a daughter, now abandoned.

Lilly of the Valley circles a stranger's porch—
a road not taken, avoided even now.

Silk peonies cling to a thin wrist,
persistent until the last toast.

Yellow petals flutter in the wind—
always, yellow lilies in a cold wind.

Your valentine rose, months later,
dries in the vase, unflinching.

The Sum of the Parts
—After Mark Doty

My river bank—mine,
I claim it, this mix
of sand and rock,

moss-speckled trees
dappled sunlight
shimmered fairies.

I breathe
river mud, crawdads,
skipping stones,

fish that nibble me
        nibble me.

I am the river—
the whirls and bends,
eddies and marshes.

I care for her gently,
risk crossings I know
like I know my heart beats.

And that is the strength—
the quiet things of the river
memories that soothe my dreams

the stillness of a sycamore leaf,
a stick, a feather from the heron
that shadows overhead.

And what I have learned
that eludes me even now,

I hold back from all
but the river.

And if we say *river*,
open our mouths—
she speaks her name.

A Poem about You

The curl of a tendril
      toward the sun—
          a seedling
            which I could not thin—
reminds me
      of how you bloom:
          tenacious.
          No hothouse flower,
you root to bedrock.

Last night you told me
      you understood—
         that's   a rare gift
      to a mother
          who wishes
              [what]
that she understood, too.

On Learning

My father dug the potatoes with a pitchfork, spread them single layer in the cellar on old newspaper, threw clumps of straw over the strawberries, hauled in a load of dry manure, spread it in the garden and tilled it under. He hosed the grass from the mower, drained the dirty oil, filled it with new, cleaned the spark plug with the round wire brush on the grinder bolted to the workbench, pulled off the mower blade and clamped it tight, filed it until the edges were sharp, wiped the blade and the hoe and the shovel with an old undershirt dipped in engine oil. He brought down storm windows from the garage rafters, washed them with vinegar, slid them into the aluminum frames on the first- and second-story windows, checked the furnace, pulled the front porch swing chains until snug against the bead-board ceiling, unhooked the garden hose, wrapped it in a tight loop around hand and elbow, raked the last of the leaves into a pile with dead tomato plants and burned it all, added the ashes to the garden rows. Now years since his last winter, I drag a finger across a window caked with dust, the yard mounds in leaves.

Appalachia Elegy

I slide through silver leaves
from maples rooted to rock,

leaned over like ancient ladies
of mottled bark—grey then black,

brown then tan—until I am
clinging to a branch, and the limestone

fractured by the percussion
is blast-scooped with the mountain,

and machines that shudder the ground
push the rock flat over the stream—until green

retreats and only grey remains crushed
flat with a layer of red dirt,

a desert in place of ancient hill
my inward eye still sees.

Finally, malls concrete over
the false prairie in progress

until the vein of black burns
and I am wrapped in twisted copper,

torn in half.

At the End of Winter

We cover the trees before a frost.
The old floral sheet clashes
with the peach tree blooms thickening on the branches.

The first tree is obstinate, sends out the pink early,
before spring, before the last freeze.
I prune it to the bone, but it refuses to be molded,

insists on shoots pointed toward the sky, even though
they will break and split—down to the heart.

To the Man Who Saved the Fledgling This Morning

On a spring workday morning, early,
a line of cars caterpillared through four stop signs
on a neighborhood lane. I thought there was a wreck
when you climbed out of your blue truck in the mist.
But you stopped traffic with an outstretched hand,
bent over, and with wide-spread fingers,
shooed the flutter of wings from the road.

For a moment, all of us alone in our cars
stopped thinking about getting to work,
preparation for a 9 o'clock meeting,
the onslaught of radio morning news.
We saw the vines trail in the oak,
the tiger lilies in the ditch, the way the fog
swallowed everything beyond.

The Concert

That morning a heavy branch split,
leaned over the neighbor's backyard fence,
spared the peach trees and the asparagus,
scattered geranium blooms across the lawn.
You hired a man to cut the wood,
told him *Come tomorrow—*
tonight I have a date.

At the concert, we sat two steep rows
from the balcony railing, held hands,
listened to the band—heard only the undertone.
You grew quiet, didn't stand at the ovation—
too near the dizzying balcony.

We'll pay extra next time
for the orchestra section, look up
at guitar strings instead of down
at the woman standing near the front,
bent arms swaying overhead.

After the concert, we wandered streets,
passed the shuttered antique store
with the *Open* sign, the pottery studio
with green clay apples in the window.

When we got home, the neighbor's fence
was still intact, the tree limb had not shifted,
the scar glittered bright, weeping
sap down the trunk.

If the apples had been red,
we would have brought them home,
placed something fragile on the shelf.

Orange Beach, Gulf Shores, September 2010
"damages were limited"
—oil company executives

The first night of our vacation on the beach—
bare feet, ocean breeze, sunset—

an elderly man with a puppy:
a chocolate dachshund, sneezing sand from his nose.

Sanderlings scurried in and out of the waves
dipping beaks like feathered sewing machines.

Next morning, we woke to the sunrise—an early alarm.
Men in hazmat suits and yellow boots scooped tar balls.

We cooked breakfast: bacon, eggs, biscuits.
I set the oven timer for 10 hours instead of minutes.

The biscuits baked black, but I filled them with butter,
And you ate them anyway, washed down with milk.

Later, we watched from the balcony—two children
at the edge of the waves, their jeans wicking salt water.

I pulled my jacket close against the chill.
A dozen dolphins frolicked off shore.

Now, we stay close to home. Walk small town streets.
Sometimes I forget I have ocean in my veins,

pull oiled seaweed from my hair.

Transplant

I take dirt
      under my fingernails,
           a strand of Kudzu around an ankle,
coal dust ground into calloused feet, gospel
music sung in coal camp meeting houses,

stay away,
      sever all connections
           like snakes
in the garden, chopped with a hoe,
and slung into the woods.

Years later—
      healing my wounds,
           stirring embers
below a small November sky,
I watch for bear and shooting stars

like my mother
      used to
           on the back porch.
I retrace my steps, sift through memories,
search for connections to people I don't know.

I still can't
      sell what I own.
           There's no one left
to buy. I'm between two worlds—
stay away from both.

In Defense of Small Towns
—After Oliver de la Paz

When I remember, I remember
old white houses with giant ferns
hanging on wrap-around porches,
bicycle rides on country roads,
the tractor's drive when my foot slipped
on the brake and almost took out the gate.
I remember sheepdogs stalking
the cowering herd, the snap of the whip,
daydreaming in cemeteries, leaning
on old tombstones, watching
headlights climb the bedroom wall
as cars passed in the night, finding
a dead dog chained in a copse of trees,
riding horses—once a Tennessee Walker—
but mostly bareback wearing shorts
on ponies and the coarse blond hairs
clinging to my sweaty legs.
I remember stories, stories about bulls
pinning men against barn walls,
and Amish girls sneaking out
knowing they would be beat
with a log chain if found out.
I remember the secrets, how they
needed us, how we needed them.

In the Frame

Picture a crime scene, but without the tape:
six empty chairs arch an overgrown yard,
a pink doll stroller waits for a blonde girl,
the grass swallows empty bottles, pool toys—
but no pool—a cardboard box of crackers.
A gray laundry basket bakes in July sun.
I can almost see the women—sisters—
storytellers all. A strand of laughter
drifts toward me with the cigarette smoke.
An artist would despair at the palette:
coral cushions, yellow toys, the violet
of the sagging Halloween wreath fastened
to the door, ultramarine reflection
on your car window as you drive away.

Sky Gazing

The sun shrunk
until it slivered
and we waited
under a canopy
in the back yard
with iced tea and chips,
cardboard glasses,
steamer baskets—
grateful for a reason
to look away
to the sky.

The tree frogs
began their keening
in the mid-day dusk,
and the neighbor's dogs howled—
didn't they? We would have
all felt silly at home alone,
peering at shadows
through a colander.

On the Hiking Trail to Rainbow Falls
    "Deadly wildfires ripped through the foothills of the Great
    Smoky Mountains"
        —New York Times, November 29, 2016

Wild grapevines thick as arms
cluster and vein up oak and birch
trellising across the raddled spruce,
thin cold air freshens my nostrils.
The only sound: the mountain stream
following itself over mossy rocks
ghosting the boulder-lined trail
split by roots from long surrendered trees
rotting on the forest floor, cushioned by dry leaves.
The fall colors—almost here, almost gone—
dim in the dry autumn. Ferns fan down the bank.

After the fire, smoke drifts from my dreams,
set on an automatic loop, the heat crawls up my chest,
ashes spark with the wind, blacken my palms with tree soot,
my neck sweats. All that remains, a leaf
picked as a reminder of the exact red
pressed in a notebook, one lobe folded down,
veined like my father's hand
I used to trace with my fingertips.
Some call peace the interval between wars.
What if peace feels like war?
What if the break between wars won't stop the burning?

What Lies Beneath

Write down what simmers
under rotting tree limbs, old tires,
unmatched shoes, a broken doll,
wreckage of all sorts.

Don't forget the bodies—
the current stripping away flesh
until only polished bones remain.

How else to encounter
what lies beneath?

Pamela Hirschler's poems have appeared in numerous journals, including *Pine Mountain Sand & Gravel, Still: The Journal, The Heartland Review, The Pikeville Review, Talking River,* and *Kudzu.* She has also been published in the anthologies *Her Limestone Bones* and *This Wretched Vessel.* Her work was included in the 2018-2019 Women of Appalachia Project reading series, and she was a 2018 finalist for *The Heartland Review*'s Joy Bale Boone Poetry Prize. Hirschler holds a BA in English from Morehead State University and a Master of Fine Arts in Poetry from Drew University. She is past president and webmaster for the Kentucky State Poetry Society and a former board member of the Green River Writers. After a 20-year career in information technology, Pamela lives with her husband in Frankfort, Kentucky. Visit her website at www.pamelahirschler.com.

www.ingramcontent.com/pod-product-compliance
Lightning Source LLC
LaVergne TN
LVHW040118080426
835507LV00041B/1774